1 Corinthians:
Leader Guide

1 CORINTHIANS:
SEARCHING THE DEPTHS OF GOD

1 Corinthians

978-1-5018-9143-4

978-1-5018-9144-1 eBook

1 Corinthians DVD

978-1-5018-9147-2

1 Corinthians Leader Guide

978-1-5018-9145-8

978-1-5018-9146-5 eBook

LEADER GUIDE

1 CORINTHIANS

Searching the Depths of God

JAIME CLARK-SOLES

Abingdon Press / Nashville

1 CORINTHIANS: LEADER GUIDE

Copyright © 2021 Abingdon Press

All rights reserved.

978-1-5018-9145-8

Leader Guide written by Katie Montgomery Mears

21 22 23 24 25 26 27 28 29 30 — 10 9 8 7 6 5 4 3 2 1

MANUFACTURED IN THE UNITED STATES OF AMERICA

CONTENTS

CONTENTS

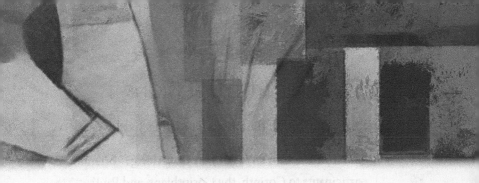

INTRODUCTION

In *1 Corinthians: Searching the Depths of God*, Jaime Clark-Soles (Professor of New Testament and Altshuler Distinguished Teaching Professor at Perkins School of Theology, Southern Methodist University) explores one of the most gripping books of the Bible, Paul's first letter to the Corinthians. The Corinthian Christ followers were trying a new social experiment—Christian community—in the midst of a first-century "sin city." Not unlike the church today, this community dealt with factions, sexual immorality, gender issues, money issues, theological questions, lawsuits, problems in worship, and problems in leadership.

Jaime Clark-Soles in her book explores these topics and the awe-inspiring, breathtaking world of the first-century church. Examining the teachings of Paul, she addresses church history, the Logic of the Cross, spiritual gifts, death, afterlife and the resurrection, human sexuality, and the joys and challenges of living in community with the ultimate goal of helping people apply the lessons of 1 Corinthians to their own faith.

This Leader Guide is designed to help leaders guide a group through a six-session study of 1 Corinthians informed by Jaime's book. The Leader Guide contains quotations from her book that can serve as prompts for discussion, but groups will gain the most when this guide is accompanied by reading 1 Corinthians alongside Jaime's book.

7

ABOUT THE SESSIONS

Here is an overview of the six sessions in this Leader Guide:

- **"Session 1—Can't We All Just Get Along?"** orients participants to Corinth, the Corinthians, and Paul's correspondence with them; it also introduces the concept of the Logic of the Cross, which is the Logic of Love.
- **"Session 2—Relationship Status: It's Complicated"** helps participants understand Paul's ethical framework and eschatology through the lens of sexual relationships.
- **"Session 3—Freedom: From What, For What?"** discusses more about how the ancient cultural worship practices in place in Corinth affected the witness and lived experience of new Christ followers there and reflect on how their own behaviors might be a stumbling block for others.
- **"Session 4—Gathering for Good"** explores three major challenges for the gatherings of the early Corinthian community—whether or not men and women should wear hats in church when they prophesy, the hierarchy imposed on the Lord's Supper, and the tendency toward individualism with spiritual gifts—and the deeper implications of these behaviors.
- **"Session 5—Talented and Gifted"** encourages participants to reflect on the value of spiritual gifts, how individual gifts enhance the body of Christ, and the calling to name and highlight others' gifts.
- **"Session 6—Bodies This Side of the Grave and Beyond (and In Between)"** introduces participants to three models of suffering; it also explores the questions of life after death, especially in terms of what happens to a person's physical body.

Each of the six session plans includes:

- Stated goals for you to keep in mind as you lead discussions.
- Selections of 1 Corinthians from the New Revised Standard Version Bible (NRSV) and New International Version (NIV).
- Extensive discussion questions to facilitate participants' engagement with both the biblical text and Jaime's book. You may not have time or desire to use all of the questions; choose the ones most interesting and/or relevant to your group.
- Opening and closing prayers to ground your sessions in an atmosphere of worship.

TIPS FOR ONLINE MEETINGS

Meeting online is a great option for a number of situations. During a time of a public-health hazard, such as the COVID-19 pandemic, online meetings are a welcome opportunity for folks to talk together while seeing one another's faces. Online meetings can also expand the "neighborhood" of possible group members, because people can log in from just about anywhere in the world. This also gives those who do not have access to transportation or who prefer not to travel at certain times of day the chance to participate.

There are a number of platforms for online meetings. Google has two products, one called Google Hangouts and one called Google Meet. You need a Google account to use them, and that account is free. At this time, there is no time limit for these meetings.

Another popular option is Zoom. This platform is used quite a bit by businesses. If your church has an account, this can be a good medium. Individuals can obtain free accounts, but those offer meetings of no longer than 40 minutes long. For longer meetings (which you will want for this study), you must pay for an account.

Some other platforms: GoToMeeting, Web Meeting, Microsoft Teams, and others. Search the internet for "web conferencing software," and you will probably find a link to top-ten rating sites that can help you choose.

- **Training and practice**
  ◊ Choose a platform and practice using it, so you are comfortable with it. Engage in a couple of practice runs with another person.
  ◊ In advance, teach participants how to log in. Explain that you will send them an invitation via e-mail, and that it will include a link for them to click at the time of the meeting.
  ◊ For those who do not have internet service, let them know they may call into the meeting. Provide the number and let them know that there is usually a unique phone number for each meeting.
  ◊ During the training meeting, show participants the basic tools available for them to use. They can learn others as they feel more confident. Make the meeting fun by showing some amusing content, such as the Facebook page Church Humor (www.facebook.com/ChurchLOL/).

- **The real meetings**
  ◊ **Early invitations.** Send out invitations at least a week in advance. Many meeting platforms enable you to do this through their software.
  ◊ **Early log in.** Participants should log in at least ten minutes in advance to test their audio and video connections.
  ◊ **Talking/not talking.** Instruct participants to keep their mics muted during the meeting, so extraneous noise from their location does not interrupt the meeting. This includes chewing or yawning sounds, which can be embarrassing!

◊ **Signaling.** When it is time for discussion, participants can unmute themselves. However, ask them to raise their hand or wave when they are ready to share, so you can call on them. Give folks a few minutes to speak up. They may not be used to conversing in web conferences.

◊ **Worship.** If there is any worship liturgy, send it out in advance. Participants can download it and follow it during the meeting. You may also share your screen so participants can follow along that way. Keep in mind that this approach will limit your ability to show other visuals during that time. Remember if you have interactive parts of opening and closing liturgies, there are ways to manage who speaks and when. Most of these platforms make it difficult for more than one speaker or singer at different locations to stay "in sync" with one another due to the lag time. Everyone should be muted while listening to prayers and litanies. They should still participate aloud in their location, however. For music, it may be better to share an online video that has music of favorite hymns. Participants can sing along in their locations (with their mics muted). A search may help you identify those you like.

◊ **Show and tell.** Make good use of visual media, since it is available on these platforms and audio-only can get boring. Consider choosing and showing artwork, creche scenes, cartoons, children's drawings, and so on. Prepare décor such as a lit candle or other suitable items to be visible with you. When you feel adept at doing so, you can show appropriate videos you find on the internet. Consider posting related art or wall hangings in the background of the room where you are participating.

Session 1
CAN'T WE ALL JUST GET ALONG?

SESSION GOALS

This session's reading, discussion, reflection, and prayer will equip participants to

- develop a deeper understanding of the culture and background of first-century Corinth and the new community of believers gathered there;
- learn about the upside-down Logic of the Cross;
- understand the context of the various factions that were driving the Corinthians apart and consider the value of Christian unity.

SUGGESTED LEADER PREPARATION

- Before your first session, set aside enough time to read 1 Corinthians 1–4 in a single sitting, at least once. Make notes on the major topics and themes. Try outlining the chapters and summarizing them in your own words. The more you immerse yourself in the scripture, the better prepared you will be to help participants study each of its parts in the context of the whole.

- Carefully read the introduction and chapter 1 of *1 Corinthians: Searching the Depths of God* by Jaime Clark-Soles. Note any material you need or want to research further before the session.

- Have on hand Bible dictionaries and concordances (and/or identify trusted online equivalents), a variety of Bible translations for participants to use (recommended), and pencils/pens and paper. If you are in touch with the people likely to join you for these sessions, invite them to bring their own Bibles.

- If using the video in your study, preview the session 1 segment.

BIBLICAL FOUNDATIONS

¹⁰Now I appeal to you, brothers and sisters, by the name of our Lord Jesus Christ, that all of you be in agreement and that there be no divisions among you, but that you be united in the same mind and the same purpose. ¹¹For it has been reported to me by Chloe's people that there are quarrels among you, my brothers and sisters. ¹²What I mean is that each of you says, "I belong to Paul," or "I belong to Apollos," or "I belong to Cephas," or "I belong to Christ." ¹³Has Christ been divided? Was Paul crucified for you? Or were you baptized in the name of Paul? ¹⁴I thank God that I baptized none of you except Crispus and Gaius, ¹⁵so that no one can say that you were baptized in my name. ¹⁶(I did baptize also the household of Stephanas; beyond that, I do not know whether I baptized anyone else.) ¹⁷For Christ did not send me to baptize but to proclaim the gospel, and not with eloquent wisdom, so that the cross of Christ might not be emptied of its power.

¹⁸For the message about the cross is foolishness to those who are perishing, but to us who are being saved it is the power of God. ¹⁹For it is written,

"I will destroy the wisdom of the wise,
and the discernment of the discerning I will thwart."

[26]*Consider your own call, brothers and sisters: not many of you were wise by human standards, not many were powerful, not many were of noble birth.* [27]*But God chose what is foolish in the world to shame the wise; God chose what is weak in the world to shame the strong;* [28]*God chose what is low and despised in the world, things that are not, to reduce to nothing things that are,* [29]*so that no one might boast in the presence of God.* [30]*He is the source of your life in Christ Jesus, who became for us wisdom from God, and righteousness and sanctification and redemption,* [31]*in order that, as it is written, "Let the one who boasts, boast in the Lord."*

1 Corinthians 1:10-19, 26-31

[9]*But, as it is written,*

"What no eye has seen, nor ear heard,
nor the human heart conceived,
what God has prepared for those who love him"—

[10]*these things God has revealed to us through the Spirit; for the Spirit searches everything, even the depths of God.* [11]*For what human being knows what is truly human except the human spirit that is within? So also no one comprehends what is truly God's except the Spirit of God.* [12]*Now we have received not the spirit of the world, but the Spirit that is from God, so that we may understand the gifts bestowed on us by God.* [13]*And we speak of these things in words not taught by human wisdom but taught by the Spirit, interpreting spiritual things to those who are spiritual.*

1 Corinthians 2:9-13

[3]*For you are still of the flesh. For as long as there is jealousy and quarreling among you, are you not of the flesh, and behaving*

according to human inclinations? ⁴*For when one says, "I belong
to Paul," and another, "I belong to Apollos," are you not merely
human?*

⁵*What then is Apollos? What is Paul? Servants through whom you
came to believe, as the Lord assigned to each.* ⁶*I planted, Apollos
watered, but God gave the growth.* ⁷*So neither the one who plants
nor the one who waters is anything, but only God who gives the
growth.* ⁸*The one who plants and the one who waters have a
common purpose, and each will receive wages according to the labor
of each.* ⁹*For we are God's servants, working together; you are God's
field, God's building.*

¹⁰*According to the grace of God given to me, like a skilled master
builder I laid a foundation, and someone else is building on it. Each
builder must choose with care how to build on it.* ¹¹*For no one can
lay any foundation other than the one that has been laid; that foundation is Jesus Christ.*

1 Corinthians 3:3-11

AS YOUR GROUP GATHERS

Welcome participants. Ask them to introduce themselves and to talk
briefly about what they hope to gain from this study of 1 Corinthians. Be
ready to talk about your personal interest in and hopes for the study as
well.

In the introduction to the book, Jaime Clark-Soles describes 1 Corinthians as "the church's book" because it addresses the issues the newly
formed Christian church is having in terms of their relationships with
one another and as witnesses for Jesus Christ. As we will see in this study,
Paul is compelled to write to them because of his deep love for this community that he founded. In his second letter to the Corinthians, he writes,
"I will most gladly spend and be spent for you" (2 Corinthians 12:15).

Ask the group:

- Is there anyone for whom you would gladly spend and be spent?
- What does it look like on a practical level to be spent for someone?

Pray this prayer or one in your own words:

Eternal God, we are grateful to be able to study your word in community. We pray that your Spirit would be with us, opening our ears that we might hear a new message from you and softening our hearts that we might be drawn closer to you through this study. Amen.

VIDEO

After viewing the first session of the video, ask your group the following questions:

- Do you idealize the early church, imagining that it must have been easier to be a Christian in the first century than it is now?
- What is the positive role of disagreement in a Christian community? When is conflict not a bad thing?
- How can you build up other people for the good of Jesus rather than focusing on conflict?
- What strategies for reconciliation do Jaime and George make in the video? Do you have any others that you would add to that list?

WHO ARE THE CORINTHIANS AND WHY DID PAUL WRITE TO THEM?

As Jaime mentions in her book, Corinth was an important city in Paul's time. It was formerly a Greek city but was captured and completely destroyed in 146 BCE by the Roman General Lucius Mummius. It sat as a pile of ashes for about one hundred years until Julius Caesar decided to rebuild the city in 44 BCE as a Roman colony. It was selected to be the seat of its province, which means it was the center of a lot of business and culture, leading to a number of new people settling there. Additionally, Corinth was located on a coastal inlet and had two ports, which allowed for passage between the Ionian Sea and the Aegean Sea, making it an important site for trade. In Jaime's words, "Corinth was a multicultural, multiethnic, multilingual, multireligious place, not unlike our own."

Since Paul was the one who established the church in Corinth, it's only natural that when disagreements and challenges arose in the church community, they would turn to Paul for help. In this occasional letter, Paul addresses a number of conflicts threatening to bring division.

Ask the group:

- If you could write a letter to your church, what are the main issues you'd want to address? (Note to the group leader: make a list of the issues mentioned by the participants. You will use this list in the closing activity.)

THE LOGIC OF THE CROSS

In 1 Corinthians 1:18, Paul writes that those who are perishing and those who are being saved view the cross differently.

- To whom do you think Paul is referring when he talks about "those who are perishing"?
- Contrast their response to the cross with those who are being saved. Why does the cross mean different things to each of those groups?

18

- In 1 Corinthians 1:19, Paul quotes Isaiah's prophecy. Have someone in your group look up Isaiah 29:14 and read it aloud to the group.
- Using 1 Corinthians 1:19-25 as a reference, how has God fulfilled that prophecy?

Jaime writes, "What's at stake for Paul here is that we live with intention, on purpose, logically—not just with *any* intention or purpose or logic, but with that which derives from the values on display in the life, death, and resurrection of Jesus."

- What are these values?
- Read 1 Corinthians 1:10. How does this frame the concept of the logic that Paul is talking about?
- Living out these values concretely means redefining power and weakness, wisdom and foolishness, and the importance of unity. As a group, talk about how the world defines power, weakness, wisdom, foolishness, and unity. How are those definitions different for Christians?
- What does this logic look like, practically speaking, in your own life? Encourage group members to share specific examples.

A SPIRIT OF UNITY

One of the primary conflicts that Paul addresses right at the beginning of the letter is the division between the factions of followers. They have divided themselves into distinctive groups that adhere to the teachings of specific apostles—Paul, Apollos, Cephas (Peter)—rather than being united in their faith in Jesus. Paul asks them, "Has Christ been divided?" (1 Corinthians 1:13).

- What factions do you get caught up in?
- Why do you think Paul wanted to play down his role in baptizing people?
- What does Paul want the Corinthians to focus on instead?

Jaime writes, "When we understand that we are, by God's design, connected to all God's creation, it means that together, we are more than we could be on our own. When we realize that, by God's design, we are each gifted in certain ways (and not in others), we can relax into that fact without envying someone else or pretending to be something we aren't."

- Are you inclined to try to do and be everything? Or do you only focus on the gifts you know you have?
- When have you been in a situation in which success was achieved only because of multiple people bringing their gifts and skills to bear on the situation?
- Paul was not an autocrat—he worked with an innumerable list of people. What is the benefit for the Kingdom of working with like-minded folks?

In her analysis of 1 Corinthians 3:1-9, Jaime notes that ultimately building the community is dependent on God. Paul and Apollos can only do so much. Have someone in your group read Mark 4:26-29.

- What does this parable remind you about our efforts as apostles?
- When people decide to follow Jesus Christ and the church grows, who should get the glory?

IS IT ESSENTIAL?

Jaime will take up this topic on a deeper level in her explanation about 1 Corinthians 8–10 (chapter 3 in her book), but she broaches in this chapter that the consideration of what is essential versus what is not essential is one of the keys to unity.

- Read 1 Corinthians 2:10. What does that scripture reveal about how we discern what is essential?
- How do you react to the quotation, "In essentials, unity; in non-essentials, liberty; in all things, love"?

CLOSING ACTIVITY

Remind the group members of the list they compiled of main issues they would want to address in a letter to their church. Challenge everyone to spend time in prayer with the Holy Spirit this week discerning which of those issues are essential and which are nonessential.

Pray this prayer or one in your own words:

Gracious God, as the hymn says, we want to be one in your Spirit, that our unity may be restored, and that we'd be known by our love. We pray that you would make these our deepest longings rather than abstract ideas that are easily cast aside when things get hard. Help us to live by the Logic of Love this week so that we might put the good of the community ahead of our own selfish desires. Amen.

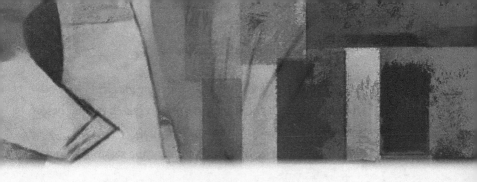

Session 2

RELATIONSHIP STATUS: IT'S COMPLICATED

SESSION GOALS

This session's reading, discussion, reflection, and prayer will equip participants to

- understand the spectrum of issues surrounding sexual relationships that were causing division in the church;
- evaluate whether something is beneficial just because it is permissible;
- learn about how Paul's understanding of eschatology impacted his ethical directives;
- use the Wesleyan Quadrilateral as a model for understanding how God would have us respond to complex or confusing issues.

SUGGESTED LEADER PREPARATION

- Carefully and prayerfully read 1 Corinthians 5–7; make notes of whatever grabs your attention most, sparks questions, or prompts new insights.

- Read chapter 2 of *1 Corinthians: Searching the Depths of God*. Note any material you need or want to research further before the session.
- If using the video in your study, preview the session 2 segment.

BIBLICAL FOUNDATIONS

¹*It is actually reported that there is sexual immorality among you, and of a kind that even pagans do not tolerate: A man is sleeping with his father's wife.* ²*And you are proud! Shouldn't you rather have gone into mourning and have put out of your fellowship the man who has been doing this?*

⁹*I wrote to you in my letter not to associate with sexually immoral people—*¹⁰*not at all meaning the people of this world who are immoral, or the greedy and swindlers, or idolaters. In that case you would have to leave this world.* ¹¹*But now I am writing to you that you must not associate with anyone who claims to be a brother or sister but is sexually immoral or greedy, an idolater or slanderer, a drunkard or swindler. Do not even eat with such people.*

¹²*What business is it of mine to judge those outside the church? Are you not to judge those inside?* ¹³*God will judge those outside. "Expel the wicked person from among you."*

1 Corinthians 5:1-2, 9-13 NIV

¹²*"All things are lawful for me," but not all things are beneficial. "All things are lawful for me," but I will not be dominated by any-thing.* ¹³*"Food is meant for the stomach and the stomach for food," and God will destroy both one and the other. The body is meant not for fornication but for the Lord, and the Lord for the body.* ¹⁴*And God raised the Lord and will also raise us by his power.* ¹⁵*Do you not know that your bodies are members of Christ? Should I therefore take the members of Christ and make them members of*

a prostitute? Never! ¹⁶*Do you not know that whoever is united to a prostitute becomes one body with her? For it is said, "The two shall be one flesh."* ¹⁷*But anyone united to the Lord becomes one spirit with him.* ¹⁸*Shun fornication! Every sin that a person commits is outside the body; but the fornicator sins against the body itself.* ¹⁹*Or do you not know that your body is a temple of the Holy Spirit within you, which you have from God, and that you are not your own?* ²⁰*For you were bought with a price; therefore glorify God in your body.*

1 Corinthians 6:12-20

¹⁷*However that may be, let each of you lead the life that the Lord has assigned, to which God called you. This is my rule in all the churches.* ¹⁸*Was anyone at the time of his call already circumcised? Let him not seek to remove the marks of circumcision. Was anyone at the time of his call uncircumcised? Let him not seek circumcision.* ¹⁹*Circumcision is nothing, and uncircumcision is nothing; but obeying the commandments of God is everything.* ²⁰*Let each of you remain in the condition in which you were called.*

1 Corinthians 7:17-20

³²*I want you to be free from anxieties. The unmarried man is anxious about the affairs of the Lord, how to please the Lord;* ³³*but the married man is anxious about the affairs of the world, how to please his wife,* ³⁴*and his interests are divided. And the unmarried woman and the virgin are anxious about the affairs of the Lord, so that they may be holy in body and spirit; but the married woman is anxious about the affairs of the world, how to please her husband.* ³⁵*I say this for your own benefit, not to put any restraint upon you, but to promote good order and unhindered devotion to the Lord.*

1 Corinthians 7:32-35

AS YOUR GROUP GATHERS

Welcome participants. Ask those who attended the first session to talk briefly about what most interested, challenged, or helped them. If they feel comfortable, encourage them to share that the Holy Spirit revealed to them this week about what was essential and nonessential on the list of issues they wrote.

In a given month, you might introduce yourself to or make small talk with people a dozen times. Because the encounters are brief, you are probably intentional with the information you convey and try to give the person the information you consider critical about yourself: marital status, job, hometown, family. In the video for this session, Jaime and Katie talk about how people are often classified, especially in churches, by their demographics, like marital status.

Ask the group members to form pairs and spend five minutes introducing themselves to each other in a few sentences, but not including marital status, job, hometown, or family information. When they are finished, ask everyone to tell the group what they discovered about their partner for the activity that they might have missed if they'd simply relied on demographic details.

Pray this prayer or one in your own words:

Merciful God, we are thankful for the gift of your Scripture. Help us to set aside the concerns that are weighing on our shoulders and distracting us from what you want to teach us. May our conversation today honor you and open us to the transforming work of your child who first loved us, Jesus Christ. Amen.

VIDEO

After viewing the second session of the video, ask your group the following questions:

- Do you relate to Katie's comment about people finding their worth in their relationship status instead of in God? What do you think Paul would say to you about that?
- How have you been able to uniquely share the gospel in different life stages?
- How can churches do a better job talking about human sexuality?

LET'S TALK ABOUT SEX

The Corinthians were having lots of problems with sex...too much (and with the wrong people) and too little (in a misguided attempt to be holy).

- In 1 Corinthians 5:1-2, Paul confronts them about a man who is having sex with his father's wife. Ask someone in your group to read Leviticus 18:8 and Deuteronomy 27:20. How should the Corinthians have responded to this situation?
- In 1 Corinthians 5:2, Paul writes that the Corinthians are arrogant about this behavior. What kinds of immorality are Christians inappropriately proud of today?
- How does one person's actions affect the others in the community? Why does Paul say they need to remove him? (reference 1 Corinthians 5:6)
- As a group, discuss your answer to Jaime's questions:

  ◊ "How much accountability is there in churches for our behavior, and how does this work in a healthy (not twisted, traumatic) way?"
  ◊ "How does your church deal with such issues?"

Jaime writes, "Christians should behave as Christ would....With every move they make with their bodies, they are to ask: Is this what

Christ would do? Is this how Jesus would interact with this person?" The Corinthians, on the other hand, believed that sex was merely physical (equating fulfilling appetites for sex with fulfilling their appetites for food in 6:13) and it led them to treat others as objects rather than as valued creation.

- How can viewing everyone through the lens of 1 Corinthians 6:19-20 help curb behavior that simply uses and discards others?

CAN I? VS. SHOULD I?

Paul's framework for this discussion is sexual behavior, but you can substitute any topic for sex and come to the same overarching question: Can I? vs. Should I? Just because you can do something doesn't always mean you should. There are two ends of the spectrum of living freely: we must ask ourselves if our behavior is edifying ("beneficial") or if it is enslaving ("dominating").

- Do you think that Christians have the right to do anything that is lawful? Why or why not?
- How does limiting your own rights benefit others?
- Paul writes, "'All things are lawful for me,' but not all things are beneficial. . . . I will not be dominated by anything" (1 Corinthians 6:12). What is the cumulative effect of giving in to worldly desires? How do those things eventually come to dominate us?
- Have you been in a situation in which you have been dominated by sin, living under its power and authority? How did it feel?

ETHICS AND THE END OF THE WORLD

Because Paul believed Jesus would return soon and that the world was nearing its end, he encouraged the Corinthians to essentially "stay put" in their lives—if they were married, great, stay married; if they were single, even better, stay single.

- Ask someone in your group to read 1 Corinthians 7:7. What do you think Paul means by "each has a particular gift from God"?
- Read 1 Corinthians 7:32-35. What was Paul's motivation for giving this advice?
- How does your eschatology (beliefs about the end of the world) affect your choices?
- If the world was ending in a year, would you change your current behaviors, habits, and beliefs? If so, what changes would you make?

WESLEYAN QUADRILATERAL

In her discussion of the slavery issue in 1 Corinthians 7, Jaime mentions using Scripture, tradition, reason, and experience as lenses. This four-pronged approach is often referred to as the Wesleyan Quadrilateral, named for John Wesley, the founder of Methodism who used this approach (though he did not codify it himself).

Paul actually models the use of the Wesleyan Quadrilateral in 1 Corinthians 15:1-19. Verse 1 attests to tradition: "the good news that I proclaimed to you, which you in turn received." Paul writes that Christ died and rose in accordance with the scriptures in verses 3-4. In verse 11, Paul tells of the Corinthians' experience: "so you have come to believe." Finally, he gives a *via negativa* argument in verses 13-19, showing how the believers used reason to fully understand the resurrection of Jesus and the dead.

- What method do you use to approach complicated situations that may, on their surface, contradict scripture?

- How does the Wesleyan Quadrilateral help you understand God's true intentions for slaves?
- How can you apply this model of discernment to other issues in your life?

CLOSING ACTIVITY

Invite the group to spend time this week in prayer thanking God for their marriage or their singleness and asking God to reveal to them how they can use their current status to share the gospel with others.

Pray this prayer or one in your own words:

Jesus, too often we take your gift of freedom and abuse it. We think that just because we are allowed to do something that it is always okay. Help us to discern which things are beneficial and which things can lead to a path of destruction, either for us or someone else. Bring our hearts back into alignment with yours so that we turn away from our self-interests, especially those that come at a cost to someone else. Amen.

Session 3

FREEDOM: FROM WHAT, FOR WHAT?

SESSION GOALS

This session's reading, discussion, reflection, and prayer will equip participants to

- study the role of situational ethics and how wisdom is meant to serve as a guide;
- discern how they may be unwittingly acting as a stumbling block in the faith journeys of other people;
- understand how Paul's "all things to all people" approach allows him to share the gospel more effectively.

SUGGESTED LEADER PREPARATION

- Carefully and prayerfully read 1 Corinthians 8–10; make notes of whatever grabs your attention most, sparks questions, or prompts new insights.
- Read chapter 3 of *1 Corinthians: Searching the Depths of God*. Note any material you need or want to research further before the session.
- If using the video in your study, preview the session 3 segment.

BIBLICAL FOUNDATIONS

¹*Now concerning food sacrificed to idols: we know that "all of us possess knowledge." Knowledge puffs up, but love builds up.* ²*Anyone who claims to know something does not yet have the necessary knowledge;* ³*but anyone who loves God is known by him.*

⁴*Hence, as to the eating of food offered to idols, we know that "no idol in the world really exists," and that "there is no God but one."* ⁵*Indeed, even though there may be so-called gods in heaven or on earth—as in fact there are many gods and many lords—*⁶*yet for us there is one God, the Father, from whom are all things and for whom we exist, and one Lord, Jesus Christ, through whom are all things and through whom we exist.*

⁷*It is not everyone, however, who has this knowledge. Since some have become so accustomed to idols until now, they still think of the food they eat as food offered to an idol; and their conscience, being weak, is defiled.* ⁸*"Food will not bring us close to God." We are no worse off if we do not eat, and no better off if we do.* ⁹*But take care that this liberty of yours does not somehow become a stumbling block to the weak.* ¹⁰*For if others see you, who possess knowledge, eating in the temple of an idol, might they not, since their conscience is weak, be encouraged to the point of eating food sacrificed to idols?* ¹¹*So by your knowledge those weak believers for whom Christ died are destroyed.* ¹²*But when you thus sin against members of your family, and wound their conscience when it is weak, you sin against Christ.* ¹³*Therefore, if food is a cause of their falling, I will never eat meat, so that I may not cause one of them to fall.*

1 Corinthians 8

¹²*If others share this rightful claim on you, do not we still more?*

Nevertheless, we have not made use of this right, but we endure anything rather than put an obstacle in the way of the gospel of Christ.

¹⁹*For though I am free with respect to all, I have made myself a slave to all, so that I might win more of them.* ²⁰*To the Jews I became as a Jew, in order to win Jews. To those under the law I became as one under the law (though I myself am not under the law) so that I might win those under the law.* ²¹*To those outside the law I became as one outside the law (though I am not free from God's law but am under Christ's law) so that I might win those outside the law.* ²²*To the weak I became weak, so that I might win the weak. I have become all things to all people, that I might by all means save some.* ²³*I do it all for the sake of the gospel, so that I may share in its blessings.*

1 Corinthians 9:12, 19-23

²³*"All things are lawful," but not all things are beneficial. "All things are lawful," but not all things build up.* ²⁴*Do not seek your own advantage, but that of the other.* ²⁵*Eat whatever is sold in the meat market without raising any question on the ground of conscience,* ²⁶*for "the earth and its fullness are the Lord's."* ²⁷*If an unbeliever invites you to a meal and you are disposed to go, eat whatever is set before you without raising any question on the ground of conscience.* ²⁸*But if someone says to you, "This has been offered in sacrifice," then do not eat it, out of consideration for the one who informed you, and for the sake of conscience—* ²⁹*I mean the other's conscience, not your own. For why should my liberty be subject to the judgment of someone else's conscience?* ³⁰*If I partake with thankfulness, why should I be denounced because of that for which I give thanks?*

³¹*So, whether you eat or drink, or whatever you do, do everything for the glory of God.* ³²*Give no offense to Jews or to Greeks or to the church of God,* ³³*just as I try to please everyone in everything I do, not seeking my own advantage, but that of many, so that they may be saved.*

1 Corinthians 10:23-33

AS YOUR GROUP GATHERS

Welcome participants. Ask those who attended the previous session to talk briefly about what in it most interested, challenged, or helped them.

This session will consider the question of whether there are things that are worth giving up so that other people will not stumble in their faith. As a group, discuss the following questions:

- Have you ever had someone ask you to give something up for them? Did you do it? Why or why not?
- What is something you would not give up for someone else?

Pray this prayer or one in your own words:

Jesus, you humbled yourself by taking the form of a human and dying on a cross. Instead of rules and righteousness, your gentle spirit drew people of all walks of life to you. Our prayer is to point people to you so that they might know your transforming love. But we know our rigidity can get in the way of people getting to know you, so we pray that you will help us to adopt your same spirit of meekness and humility. Amen.

VIDEO

After viewing the third session of the video, ask your group the following questions:

- What is the role of sacrifice and humility in community?
- Jaime and Ellen talked about how relationships require that we leave room for people and their messiness. Are you able to do this when you're holding your ideals and beliefs with a firm grasp?
- When you hold these things with a firm grasp, are you able to leave room for people and their messiness?

- How can you identify with Paul and his failure and his realization of the need for grace?
- What does it mean to you to be "all things to all people"? How can that help you share the gospel more effectively?

SITUATIONAL ETHICS

Jaime writes, "Paul is a strong proponent of situational ethics because he knows life is complex and a simplistic, one-size-fits-all rule is ineffective at best. The bedrock ethical principle for Christians is to *assess the details of the given situation from all angles and then adopt the Logic of the Cross.*"

- What do you use to guide you in the Logic of the Cross? (Holy Spirit, God's knowledge/wisdom)
- Can you think of any divisions in your church like what the Corinthian church was facing? What would happen if you tried to use a "one-size-fits-all" rule? Would that be effective? Why or why not?

DON'T BE A STUMBLING BLOCK

Paul was not at all worried that eating meat sacrificed to idols was going to cause strong believers to weaken their faith or violate their beliefs. But he was deeply concerned that their partaking in the idol meat would cause others' faith to weaken. For Paul, that was reason enough to not consume it. Even worse, they were bragging about their superior knowledge. In other words, they knew that others might be led astray by their behavior but since it didn't harm their own beliefs, they didn't care.

- Think back to when you first became a Christ follower. Was there someone who caused you to stumble in your faith? Do

35

you think the person realized that his or her behavior might be a problem?

- What are some of the "rights" that modern Christ followers exercise that may cause others to stumble?

Ask someone in your group to look up 1 Kings 14:16. Jeroboam was the king of Israel in the divided kingdom. In an effort to win loyalty from his citizens, he had two golden calves made for the people to worship, which turned them away from God. The calves, and Jeroboam himself, were stumbling blocks that prevented the people from fully following God.

- Is it the responsibility of leaders to ensure that they do not cause someone to stumble?
- What is the role of personal responsibility in a person's faith?
- What are some of the behaviors in your own life or in your church community that might be a stumbling block for someone, especially a new believer?

Ask the members of your group to each look up one of the following scriptures and read it out loud to the group. Discuss:

- What are the common themes in these passages?

  ◊ Proverbs 27:17
  ◊ Matthew 5:29-30
  ◊ Matthew 18:6
  ◊ Romans 14:1, 14, 17, 20
  ◊ 2 Corinthians 6:3
  ◊ Galatians 5:13

Jaime writes, "Be careful not to become enslaved by your liberty." There are situations in which exercising our freedom detracts from our ability to share the gospel because we refuse to meet people where

36

they are. This does not mean compromising our standards or changing our beliefs. It means that we are willing to let go of the privileges we enjoy with our freedom if they stand in the way of someone being able to relate to us or see Jesus reflected in our lives.

Being a Christ follower often involves self-sacrifice. Jesus told his followers that they must deny themselves as they take up his cross. In Matthew 25, Jesus says that the way we treat the weakest among us is the way we treat him.

Paul's admonishments had the good of the body at their core—not eating meat sacrificed to idols serves the greater good so that people don't stumble, even if there are individual members that would understand. For Paul, it's not about the members who would understand, but those who wouldn't. Putting our individual liberty above the needs of others, especially those who are new Christians or struggling with their faith, is a denial of Jesus. It is our duty, as Jaime writes, to "help each other up, not make each other fall."

- What are the signs you have become enslaved by your liberty?
- Have you been in a situation similar to the one Jaime described regarding pantyhose? How did you handle it?
- What are the hills that are worth dying on?
- Are you receptive to people pointing out when you're putting your liberties above the common good?

IMITATORS OF CHRIST

Paul models ethical behavior for his followers by imitating Christ. In 1 Corinthians 9:12, 19-23, Paul writes, "For though I am free with respect to all, I have made myself a slave to all. . . . I have become all things to all people, that I might by all means save some. I do it all for the sake of the gospel, so that I may share in its blessings" (vv. 19, 22-23).

37

Is he waffling? Is he just being a people pleaser? No, he is meeting people where they are. Just like Jesus, Paul wants to be with people rather than outside of them. Being "all things to all people" means that he looks a little more like them, but he still maintains his integrity.

- How do you influence the people around you?
- How does becoming "all things to all people" help share the gospel?

CLOSING ACTIVITY

Ask each person in the group to think of one person with whom they would like to talk about God. Challenge them to spend time in prayer seeking the Holy Spirit's guidance on how they can meet that person where they are.

Pray this prayer or one in your own words:

Gracious God, we don't want anyone to trip over us on their way to you, but we aren't always the best example. Help us to remember that other people are watching us and that our actions can either help them grow closer to you or tear them down. Soften our hearts so that we put others' needs before our own. We love you and want to honor you. Amen.

Session 4
GATHERING FOR GOOD

SESSION GOALS

This session's reading, discussion, reflection, and prayer will equip participants to

- discern what is really essential and what can be set aside;
- understand the ancient context for Paul's comments about women;
- use the presenting issue of the Lord's Supper to discuss inclusion.

SUGGESTED LEADER PREPARATION

- Carefully and prayerfully read 1 Corinthians 11 and 1 Corinthians 14:33b-36; make notes of whatever grabs your attention most, sparks questions, or prompts new insights.
- Read chapter 4 of *1 Corinthians: Searching the Depths of God.* Note any material you need or want to research further before the session.
- If using the video in your study, preview the session 4 segment.

BIBLICAL FOUNDATIONS

¹Be imitators of me, as I am of Christ.

²I commend you because you remember me in everything and maintain the traditions just as I handed them on to you. ³But I want you to understand that Christ is the head of every man, and the husband is the head of his wife, and God is the head of Christ. ⁴Any man who prays or prophesies with something on his head disgraces his head, ⁵but any woman who prays or prophesies with her head unveiled disgraces her head—it is one and the same thing as having her head shaved. ⁶For if a woman will not veil herself, then she should cut off her hair; but if it is disgraceful for a woman to have her hair cut off or to be shaved, she should wear a veil. ⁷For a man ought not to have his head veiled, since he is the image and reflection of God; but woman is the reflection of man. ⁸Indeed, man was not made from woman, but woman from man. ⁹Neither was man created for the sake of woman, but woman for the sake of man. ¹⁰For this reason a woman ought to have a symbol of authority on her head, because of the angels. ¹¹Nevertheless, in the Lord woman is not independent of man or man independent of woman. ¹²For just as woman came from man, so man comes through woman; but all things come from God. ¹³Judge for yourselves: is it proper for a woman to pray to God with her head unveiled? ¹⁴Does not nature itself teach you that if a man wears long hair, it is degrading to him, ¹⁵but if a woman has long hair, it is her glory? For her hair is given to her for a covering. ¹⁶But if anyone is disposed to be contentious—we have no such custom, nor do the churches of God.

¹⁷Now in the following instructions I do not commend you, because when you come together it is not for the better but for the worse. ¹⁸For, to begin with, when you come together as a church, I hear that there are divisions among you; and to some extent I believe it. [19]*Indeed, there have to be factions among you, for only so will it become clear who among you are genuine.* [20]*When you come together, it is not really to eat the Lord's supper.* [21]*For when the time comes to eat, each of you goes ahead with your own supper, and one goes hungry and another becomes drunk.* [22]*What! Do you not have homes to eat and drink in? Or do you show contempt for the church of God and humiliate those who have nothing? What should I say to you? Should I commend you? In this matter I do not commend you!*

[23]*For I received from the Lord what I also handed on to you, that the Lord Jesus on the night when he was betrayed took a loaf of bread,* [24]*and when he had given thanks, he broke it and said, "This is my body that is for you. Do this in remembrance of me."* [25]*In the same way he took the cup also, after supper, saying, "This cup is the new covenant in my blood. Do this, as often as you drink it, in remembrance of me."* [26]*For as often as you eat this bread and drink the cup, you proclaim the Lord's death until he comes.*

[27]*Whoever, therefore, eats the bread or drinks the cup of the Lord in an unworthy manner will be answerable for the body and blood of the Lord.* [28]*Examine yourselves, and only then eat of the bread and drink of the cup.* [29]*For all who eat and drink without discerning the body, eat and drink judgment against themselves.* [30]*For this reason many of you are weak and ill, and some have died.* [31]*But if we judged ourselves, we would not be judged.* [32]*But when we are judged by the Lord, we are disciplined so that we may not be condemned along with the world.*

[33]*So then, my brothers and sisters, when you come together to eat, wait for one another.* [34]*If you are hungry, eat at home, so that when you come together, it will not be for your condemnation. About the other things I will give instructions when I come.*

1 Corinthians 11

33b(As in all the churches of the saints, 34women should be silent in the churches. For they are not permitted to speak, but should be subordinate, as the law also says. 35If there is anything they desire to know, let them ask their husbands at home. For it is shameful for a woman to speak in church. 36Or did the word of God originate with you? Or are you the only ones it has reached?)

1 Corinthians 14:33b-36

AS YOUR GROUP GATHERS

Welcome participants. Ask those who attended the previous session to talk briefly about what in it most interested, challenged, or helped them.

One of Paul's chief concerns that this lesson will address is the responsibility of the community to avoid doing anything that might distract from the real purpose of worship. Like the discussion about idol meat last week, Paul knows that head coverings do not make the person wearing them more or less worshipful of God. But they can confuse others or cause them to question motives, distracting them from worshipping God.

Walt Disney World has hundreds of thousands of square feet of tunnels running underground that employees use to take out the trash, make costume adjustments, fix broken equipment, and get around the park. One of the goals of Walt Disney World is to transport guests to a magical place, and part of that magic of escapism is the lack of distraction.

Ask the group to share situations when they have been distracted from the purpose of something and how it affected their experience (for example, a loud conversation in a movie theater, someone wearing a view-obstructing hat in front of you at a sporting event, a bad smell in a restaurant).

Pray this prayer or one in your own words:

Everlasting God, we get so caught up in minor things that we end up missing what you actually want us to focus on, which is loving each other. Help us to stop gazing inward and focusing on petty disagreements. Instead, lift our eyes to see the people around us whom we have the opportunity to serve, to include, to love. Amen.

VIDEO

After viewing the fourth session of the video, ask your group the following questions:

- How do we, as a community of faith, voice that everyone is valued?
- When have you witnessed inequality that devalues individuals or groups like the college funding situation that Ray described?
- What does the Table represent to you?
- Ray and Jaime talked about not "majoring in the minors." What should be our most important values?

WHAT'S REALLY ESSENTIAL?

Just as Paul addressed the ethic of mutual respect and love through the presenting issue of sexual relationships in 1 Corinthians 5–7, he is using another presenting issue in these chapters to make a point. It's not about the hair; it's about the custom distracting from the gospel message.

Context matters. Ancient ideas about gender and the association of long hair with pagan cults prompted Paul to issue this warning. Though he knew that women whose heads remained uncovered during worship were no less faithful than those who covered their heads, he didn't want new Christ followers or non-followers to focus on head coverings and wonder about motives. He wanted them to focus on Jesus.

43

Jaime writes, "These issues must be considered anew in each generation, not because one way is right and one is wrong but because the *meaning* that is implied by our practices can change over time." Ultimately, this is about creating and valuing community. Consider the following questions together:

- Is our church welcoming to visitors?
- What practices do we have that feel exclusive to outsiders?
- What is our motivation for having them?
- Do we need to adjust or make outright changes to any of them?

Jaime writes, "If it's not a big deal, don't make it a big deal. On the other hand, don't stand down on issues that *are* a big deal. Learn to discern."

- How do you discern what is *adiaphora* (inconsequential, "neither-here-nor-there" things) and what is a "big deal"?
- What are some examples of modern-day *adiaphora*?

Jaime writes, "We are saved together or we are damned together.... No biblical author, from Genesis to Revelation, imagined the idea of a committed follower of God who was not part of a *community*, as messy as that has always been and always will be."

- We often think about our salvation in terms of our personal relationship with God. What does it mean to be saved together?
- What is your responsibility to your community?
- Are you tempted to leave your community when it gets messy?

A WOMAN'S PLACE

For centuries, Paul's letters have been used to prohibit women from teaching or leading in churches. A thorough reading of all of

Paul's epistles reveals that Paul partnered with women in his ministry, including Phoebe, Chloe, Priscilla, Junia, and others, using titles such as deacon and apostle to describe them. As Jaime notes, Paul is not debating in 1 Corinthians 11 *whether* women should prophesy in church, but how they should dress when doing so.

- Have you experienced churches or faith leaders using selections from Paul's writings to prevent women from teaching or leading? In light of Jaime's explanation of 1 Corinthians 14:33b-36, how would you respond?

EVERYONE IS WELCOME AT THE TABLE

One of the hallmarks of the early church is the economic boundaries that were broken—wealthy Christ followers and poor Christ followers would all join together to eat and share the Lord's Supper. The Latin root of the word "communion" is *communio*, which means "sharing in common." The problem, as Paul describes it, is that some of the members of the community begin indulging before everyone arrives, and by the time the latecomers make it, there is nothing left for them. The ones who came late were probably slaves; they had longer workdays than those who employed them. So, the gathering that is supposed to look like the upside-down kingdom of God ends up looking just like the secular dinner party happening down the street. The Lord's Supper became an occasion for self-indulgence instead of self-sacrifice.

Paul chastises them for this behavior, reminding them that Jesus nullified their hierarchies. From the poorest person to the wealthiest person, every single person is a guest at the Lord's Table. No one earned their spot on their own. Everyone is there because of Jesus.

Jaime writes, "Signing on with Jesus means committing to a community of people that includes folks you might not otherwise come across in your daily life or might not consider equal to you and probably never felt a responsibility for before."

Discuss the following questions with your group:

- What does it mean to eat the bread or drink the cup "in an unworthy manner"? (1 Corinthians 11:27)
- Jaime writes that to have the mind of Christ, you must invite others to experience abundance. How are you doing this both inside the church and in your daily life?
- When you start to feel like it's "too much trouble" or "over-the-top" to care about the needs of the people in your community, do you ask yourself why it feels annoying or exasperating? Or do you see it as an exciting, relatively easy opportunity to participate in the abundant love of God?

CLOSING ACTIVITY

Next week's lesson will include a discussion on spiritual gifts. You may want to suggest to your group members that they take a spiritual gifts inventory if they've never done that before. Ask them to bring their results to the gathering next week. One can be found at https://www.umcdiscipleship.org/spiritual-gifts-inventory/en.

Invite your group members to read chapter 5 of *1 Corinthians: Searching the Depths of God* before your next meeting.

Pray this prayer or one of your own:

Holy God, you are the one whose name is Love. You are the one who guides, the one who provides, the one who heals. You are the one who continues to form us into the likeness of Christ through your kindness that leads to repentance. We pray that you would help us to discern what's really essential and what just serves to distract us. Give us eyes to see those who might be missing from our tables, and give us hearts of courage to invite them to join us. Amen.

Session 5

TALENTED AND GIFTED

SESSION GOALS

This session's reading, discussion, reflection, and prayer will equip participants to

- recognize the value of the varied spiritual gifts and how each person's unique combination of gifts helps them share the gospel;
- understand the importance of the full body of Christ;
- think about how the actions of kindness, patience, trust, and hope demonstrate love.

SUGGESTED LEADER PREPARATION

- Carefully and prayerfully read 1 Corinthians 12–14; make notes of whatever grabs your attention most, sparks questions, or prompts new insights.
- Read chapter 5 of *1 Corinthians: Searching the Depths of God*. Note any material you need or want to research further before the session.
- If using the video in your study, preview the session 5 segment.

BIBLICAL FOUNDATIONS

⁴Now there are varieties of gifts, but the same Spirit; ⁵and there are varieties of services, but the same Lord; ⁶and there are varieties of activities, but it is the same God who activates all of them in everyone. ⁷To each is given the manifestation of the Spirit for the common good. ⁸To one is given through the Spirit the utterance of wisdom, and to another the utterance of knowledge according to the same Spirit, ⁹to another faith by the same Spirit, to another gifts of healing by the one Spirit, ¹⁰to another the working of miracles, to another prophecy, to another the discernment of spirits, to another various kinds of tongues, to another the interpretation of tongues. ¹¹All these are activated by one and the same Spirit, who allots to each one individually just as the Spirit chooses.

¹²For just as the body is one and has many members, and all the members of the body, though many, are one body, so it is with Christ. ¹³For in the one Spirit we were all baptized into one body—Jews or Greeks, slaves or free—and we were all made to drink of one Spirit.

¹⁴Indeed, the body does not consist of one member but of many. ¹⁵If the foot would say, "Because I am not a hand, I do not belong to the body," that would not make it any less a part of the body. ¹⁶And if the ear would say, "Because I am not an eye, I do not belong to the body," that would not make it any less a part of the body. ¹⁷If the whole body were an eye, where would the hearing be? If the whole body were hearing, where would the sense of smell be? ¹⁸But as it is, God arranged the members in the body, each one of them, as he chose. ¹⁹If all were a single member, where would the body be? ²⁰As it is, there are many members, yet one body. ²¹The eye cannot say to the hand, "I have no need of you," nor again the head to the feet, "I have no need of you." ²²On the contrary, the members of the body that seem to be weaker are indispensable, ²³and those members of the body that we think less honorable we clothe with greater honor, and our less respectable members are treated with greater respect; [24]whereas our more respectable members do not need this. But God has so arranged the body, giving the greater honor to the inferior member, [25]that there may be no dissension within the body, but the members may have the same care for one another. [26]If one member suffers, all suffer together with it; if one member is honored, all rejoice together with it.

[27]Now you are the body of Christ and individually members of it. [28]And God has appointed in the church first apostles, second prophets, third teachers; then deeds of power, then gifts of healing, forms of assistance, forms of leadership, various kinds of tongues. [29]Are all apostles? Are all prophets? Are all teachers? Do all work miracles? [30]Do all possess gifts of healing? Do all speak in tongues? Do all interpret? [31]But strive for the greater gifts. And I will show you a still more excellent way.

1 Corinthians 12:4-31

[1]If I speak in the tongues of men or of angels, but do not have love, I am only a resounding gong or a clanging cymbal. [2]If I have the gift of prophecy and can fathom all mysteries and all knowledge, and if I have a faith that can move mountains, but do not have love, I am nothing. [3]If I give all I possess to the poor and give over my body to hardship that I may boast, but do not have love, I gain nothing.

[4]Love is patient, love is kind. It does not envy, it does not boast, it is not proud. [5]It does not dishonor others, it is not self-seeking, it is not easily angered, it keeps no record of wrongs. [6]Love does not delight in evil but rejoices with the truth. [7]It always protects, always trusts, always hopes, always perseveres.

[8]Love never fails. But where there are prophecies, they will cease; where there are tongues, they will be stilled; where there is

knowledge, it will pass away. [9]For we know in part and we prophesy in part,[10]but when completeness comes, what is in part disappears. [11]When I was a child, I talked like a child, I thought like a child, I reasoned like a child. When I became a man, I put the ways of childhood behind me. [12]For now we see only a reflection as in a mirror; then we shall see face to face. Now I know in part; then I shall know fully, even as I am fully known.

[13]And now these three remain: faith, hope and love. But the greatest of these is love.

1 Corinthians 13 NIV

AS YOUR GROUP GATHERS

Welcome participants. Ask those who attended the previous session to talk briefly about what in it most interested, challenged, or helped them.

Ask the group members to take turns sharing hidden or unusual talents. Be prepared to share yours first in order to break the ice.

Pray this prayer or one of your own:

God, you are endlessly generous with us. Thank you for the spiritual gifts that you have given to each of us. We know that we are uniquely gifted because you have a unique purpose for each of us. Help us to recognize gifts in one another and call them out in a way that lifts up everyone around us. Help us to discern how to best use our gifts to serve you and the gospel. Amen.

VIDEO

After viewing the fifth session of the video, ask your group the following questions:

- Do you compare yourself to the saints?

- In Baranda and Jaime's conversation, they talked about the flames of passion and the flames of rage as divine sparks. What was the last thing that got you really excited, either positively or negatively? What do you think God was trying to tell you through that emotion?
- How can you follow that divine spark without burning out or burning others out?
- How do you acknowledge others' gifts?
- Do you feel competitive when someone has a gift that you do not have? How do you deal with that feeling?

SPIRITUAL GIFTS

If your group members took the spiritual gifts inventory that was suggested at the end of the last gathering, invite them to share their gifts and their reactions to them. Did they find their results surprising? disappointing? encouraging? Why?

Often, people place higher value on certain spiritual gifts, especially those that are more obvious or noticeable to others, but Paul says that all gifts are important and necessary.

Jaime writes, "I am dumbstruck by the number of people who (a) don't recognize their gifts or (b) don't understand the value of their gifts for the wider world. This should remind us all how important it is both to discover our own gifts (we *all* have them) and to *name* the gifts of others and not just assume they know."

- Before you took the spiritual gifts inventory, did you recognize your spiritual gifts? Did you need someone to point them out to you or did you become aware of them on your own?
- Has the awareness of your spiritual gifts affected your choice of career or hobbies?

- Do you recognize others' gifts? If so, do you tell them?

The gifts that Paul lists in 1 Corinthians 12:8-10 include wisdom, knowledge, faith, healing, miracles, prophecy, discernment, and tongues. The gifts that Paul lists later in the chapter (vv. 28-30) include apostle, prophet, teacher, miracles, healings, assistance, administration/leadership, and tongues.

- Ask your group members to look up the following verses and read them out loud:

  ◊ Romans 12:6-8
  ◊ Ephesians 4:11
  ◊ 1 Peter 4:11

- How do all of these lists compare to each other? Why do you think they have different gifts on them?
- What would you add?

Jaime writes, "Paul lists faith as a gift, which implies that not everyone will have it."

- Do you think this means that faith is not available to some people?
- What is the gift of faith and how is it different than professing faith in Jesus?

THE IMPORTANCE OF THE FULL BODY OF CHRIST

Have you ever been to the symphony? Before the orchestra begins its performance, the musicians tune their individual instruments. When they start, you might hear only one kind of instrument, and then a second kind begins playing, and a third. And during this time, it sounds like a cacophony. It is discordant. The musicians are only concerned with the tuning on their own instrument and they are not playing in tandem. Some instruments (like the percussion) aren't even playing at all, so that adds to the sense that something is off. But when the conductor begins the performance, they all begin to play together in tandem and the resulting sound is a harmony, not a cacophony.

In the same way, our Christian community is a symphony. Just like there is a sense that something is off when an instrument is missing, the body of Christ is discordant without certain people.

- Have you ever experienced the feeling that something is off when someone is missing from your community?

Jaime writes, "Interdependence is fundamental; when one body part is affected, the whole body is affected." If you've ever broken your toe, you can relate to this. The pain is centered in your foot, but your whole body is consumed by it because you force yourself to walk differently, which takes a bit of concentration until it becomes a pattern. You might even start to feel some aches in your hips or your uninjured leg because you are overcompensating. The injured part of the body is small (a toe!) but the rest of the body is affected.

- Jaime asks the reader whether this statement describes us: "If one member suffers, all suffer together with it." What do you think? Does that describe your church or Christian community?
- Who are the people who are typically thought to be the more valued members of the community? Who is often less valued?
- Can you think of an example of an unexpected person being an important part of a group?

53

Jaime writes, "It can be freeing to recognize that we have specific God-given strengths.... We don't need to strive to be what we were not created to be." The greatest benefit to being in Christian community is that we don't have to carry the torch all by ourselves. We are able to lean on other people when we are tired or weak, or if we realize that we are not skilled at a particular aspect of our work. The message that we often get from our culture is that we have to be able to do everything on our own (think of the awe that you hear in people's voices when they exclaim, "How does she do it all!"). But Paul's message for us is that we are meant to work together in community and benefit from one another's strengths and skills.

- Are the gifts of the members of your community being used in a way that is helpful to others?
- Do you feel pressure to do it all by yourself?
- Do you struggle to do things that just don't fall in your areas of strength?
- Is there someone that you can identify and partner with that might have a strength that you don't have?

THE LOVE CHAPTER

Elitism...divisions over teaching...sexual immorality...meat sacrificed to idols...confusion over spiritual gifts...exclusion from the Lord's Supper...conduct in church gatherings...

The list of issues in the Corinthian church seems to go on and on. And yet, these problems didn't even seem to be apparent to the majority of the members of the church. In fact, they spent their time boasting about their spiritual gifts—prophesying, speaking in tongues, and their great wisdom.

Paul spends a lot of time in his letter outlining all of the issues in the Corinthian church—he chastises them for their behavior, and he offers practical instruction on how they should act. But it is in the climax of the letter that he gets to the ultimate solution: he calls them to love. That is really where his instruction was headed all along. Love that comes from unity in the Spirit solves the division that the church was facing.

- How do you define *love*?

According to Paul, love is the solution for all corporate church issues. Paul's ethic of love asks, "Does it help the other?" Even though prophecy and tongues have their place, they do not build up the church like love does. This kind of love is exhibited in action words: being patient, being kind, rejoicing in truth, trusting, hoping, enduring.

- What do all of these characteristics of love have in common? (reference 1 Corinthians 10:24)
- Which of these actions comes most naturally to you? With which do you struggle?
- Paul wants the Corinthian church to identify themselves as Christians in the midst of their culture—by the kind of love that transforms a community. How can we answer the call to the kind of love that Paul writes about in 1 Corinthians 13? Invite the group to share some practical ideas.

Will there be challenges when we answer the gospel call to love our neighbors? Of course. But Paul didn't say that it could be put on the back burner if it seemed inconvenient. In fact, it can be argued that it is rarely convenient to be kind, or to not give in to jealousy, or to be long-suffering—all qualities of Christian love.

CLOSING ACTIVITY

Give each person a note card or a half sheet of paper and have them write out 1 Corinthians 13:4-7, substituting their own name where it says "love." Ask them to stick it on their bathroom mirror and read through it each morning as a reminder of God's calling on our lives to live out love.

Pray this prayer or one of your own:

Jesus, you not only show us love, but you are love. You are patient, kind, and forgiving. Fill us with your love so that we might share it with others. Help us to model our lives after yours so that we would always have our arms open wide, welcoming people in with grace and mercy. Amen.

Session 6

Bodies This Side of the Grave and Beyond (and In Between)

Session Goals

This session's reading, discussion, reflection, and prayer will equip participants to

- develop a deeper appreciation of the importance of an embodied existence;
- refine and articulate their own understandings of impairment, disability, cure, and healing;
- learn about three models of understanding physical suffering, including the consequences of adhering to the various models;
- consider what happens to our bodies after death.

Suggested Leader Preparation

- Carefully and prayerfully read 1 Corinthians 15–16; make notes on whatever grabs your attention most, sparks questions, or prompts new insights.

- Read chapter 6 of *1 Corinthians: Searching the Depths of God*. Note any material you need or want to research further before the session.
- If using the video in your study, preview the session 6 segment.

BIBLICAL FOUNDATIONS

[12]But if it is preached that Christ has been raised from the dead, how can some of you say that there is no resurrection of the dead? [13]If there is no resurrection of the dead, then not even Christ has been raised. [14]And if Christ has not been raised, our preaching is useless and so is your faith. [15]More than that, we are then found to be false witnesses about God, for we have testified about God that he raised Christ from the dead. But he did not raise him if in fact the dead are not raised. [16]For if the dead are not raised, then Christ has not been raised either. [17]And if Christ has not been raised, your faith is futile; you are still in your sins. [18]Then those also who have fallen asleep in Christ are lost. [19]If only for this life we have hope in Christ, we are of all people most to be pitied.

[20]But Christ has indeed been raised from the dead, the firstfruits of those who have fallen asleep. [21]For since death came through a man, the resurrection of the dead comes also through a man. [22]For as in Adam all die, so in Christ all will be made alive. [23]But each in turn: Christ, the firstfruits; then, when he comes, those who belong to him. [24]Then the end will come, when he hands over the kingdom to God the Father after he has destroyed all dominion, authority and power. [25]For he must reign until he has put all his enemies under his feet. [26]The last enemy to be destroyed is death. [27]For he "has put everything under his feet." Now when it says that "everything" has been put under him, it is clear that this does not include God himself, who put everything under Christ. [28]When he has done this, then the Son himself will be made subject to him who put everything under him, so that God may be all in all.

[35]But someone will ask, "How are the dead raised? With what kind of body will they come?"

[50]I declare to you, brothers and sisters, that flesh and blood cannot inherit the kingdom of God, nor does the perishable inherit the imperishable. [51]Listen, I tell you a mystery: We will not all sleep, but we will all be changed—[52]in a flash, in the twinkling of an eye, at the last trumpet. For the trumpet will sound, the dead will be raised imperishable, and we will be changed. [53]For the perishable must clothe itself with the imperishable, and the mortal with immortality. [54]When the perishable has been clothed with the imperishable, and the mortal with immortality, then the saying that is written will come true: "Death has been swallowed up in victory."

[55]"Where, O death, is your victory?
Where, O death, is your sting?"

[56]The sting of death is sin, and the power of sin is the law. [57]But thanks be to God! He gives us the victory through our Lord Jesus Christ.

1 Corinthians 15:12-28, 35, 50-57 NIV

AS YOUR GROUP GATHERS

Welcome participants. Ask those who attended the previous session to talk briefly about what most interested, challenged, or helped them.

Pray this prayer or one of your own:

God of all, we are often too quick to dismiss people who are different from us. We don't take the time to learn more about them or develop a relationship. And yet we know that they are just as important to you as we are. And so we pray that your Spirit would guide us in our time together today, helping us to become more faithful disciples who love and include everyone we meet. Amen.

VIDEO

After viewing the sixth session of the video, ask your group the following questions:

- As Mireya mentioned in the video, people often don't realize that they are being exclusive. What can we do to be aware of our tendencies to exclude people?
- How can we do a better job of including all bodies in leadership in our communities and churches? Invite the group to offer specific ideas.
- What do you think of Mireya's mother's statement: "We don't throw people away; God doesn't throw people away."
- Have you had a mystical spiritual experience?
- Invite participants to share their experiences with the Day of the Dead or All Saints Day with the group.

EMBODIMENT

The word *body* (*sōma*) appears 35 times in 1 Corinthians. Some of those references refer to metaphorical bodies—that is, "the body of Christ." But many more of the references are to non-metaphorical bodies—that is, living, breathing human bodies. This is clearly an important concept for Paul. In his view, though we can use our bodies for harm, an embodied existence—having a body—is a good thing. We can use our bodies to act in a way that brings glory to God, and bodies participate in the resurrection.

Invite the participants to discuss these questions:

- Do you have a generally positive or negative view of embodiment?
- What do you do with your body that gives you a sense of identity? (for example, paint, garden, take care of a loved one)

- When you consider those things, does it change your view of embodiment? In what way?
- Which of your senses brings you the most joy? What do you think your life would be like without that sense that comes with your embodiment?

Jaime addresses the difference between physical impairment and disability, as well as the difference between curing and healing. What do you think of these distinctions? Were they surprising to you?

- Not everything is healed by God on this earth. Have you ever experienced a time in which you or someone you love isn't physically cured but they are healed? What did that look like?

THREE MODELS OF SUFFERING

For all that is good about them, one of the realities of bodies is that they can experience physical unhealth and suffering. What do we mean when we say we boast in our sufferings? We know that Paul doesn't just accept the thorn in his flesh (his suffering) as he goes to God three times to get rid of it. When we are full of ourselves and try to do everything by ourselves, we don't leave any room for God and the power of the Holy Spirit to work in our lives. Conversely, when we are weak and have deep spaces of emptiness, we have room for God to work in and through our lives.

In her discussion of bodily suffering, Jaime outlines three models of suffering that are found in Dr. Susan Garrett's essay, "Paul's Thorn and Cultural Models of Affliction."[*]

---

* Susan R. Garrett, chap. 6: "Paul's Thorn and Cultural Models of Affliction," in *The Social World of the First Christians: Essays in Honor of Wayne A. Meeks*, ed. L. Michael White and O. Larry Yarbrough (Minneapolis, MN: Fortress Press, 1995), 82–99.

The Job model features Satan in the role of tempter who "uses suffering to lead the righteous astray from single-minded commitment to God." It assumes that human righteousness prompts satanic attacks, that the suffering is Satan's contest, and that Satan and God have an ambiguous relationship.

- What are the four ways that Jaime suggests we respond to suffering in this model?
- Have you been tempted to turn your back on God when you or someone you love has experienced bodily suffering?
- What helped you keep your faith or brought you back to it?

The Paideia model imagines God as a parent who tests the parent's beloved children in order to teach them. It is meant to build character, correct, purify, and prepare one for accountability.

- What is the appropriate response to suffering in this model?
- How can you strike a balance between suffering that builds character and suffering that crushes? What are the long-term effects of each of those results?

The Cross model entails a "lowliness now but exaltation later" approach in which people are set free from their ego and self-centeredness so they might live by the humility of God. When it is apparent that Paul will not be physically cured, he is left with two options—to be defeated and give up or to make meaning of the suffering by relying on Christ's strength.

- How does this relate to the Logic of the Cross?
- What would it look like in your own life to take up this cross model in your suffering?

WHAT HAPPENS WHEN WE DIE?

Jaime writes that when you fall down on your knees and have a hole in your heart when someone dies, that's a holy reaction and one that God shares because Death (capitalized by Jaime because Paul personifies Death) is the last great enemy. However, Paul makes four points about death in 1 Corinthians 15 that give us reason for hope:

1. **Death is not ultimate.** As Christians, we take death seriously, but because of our belief in resurrection and immortality through Jesus, we know that death is not the final word.
2. **God wins—completely.** Paul does not write of an everlasting fiery hell because he attests that God will be "all in all" or "everything to everyone." God's faithfulness will overcome people's faithlessness.
3. **Embodiment is still good, eternally.** After Jesus's resurrection, he met two disciples on the road to Emmaus and had dinner with them. He ate breakfast on the beach with the disciples. He let Thomas touch him. Mary Magdalene clung to him. He was able to do these things because he was embodied, just as we will be after we are resurrected. God created bodies and they are good.
4. **The redemption of *all* creation.** Perfect unity with God after the general resurrection will include all of creation, not just humans.

Ask the group:

*   What questions do you have about what happens after you die?
*   Are you more concerned about the answers to these questions because you want to know what will happen to you, or because you want to know what is already happening for the people you love that have passed away? Or both?

CLOSING ACTIVITY

In her conclusion, Jaime encourages readers to write an ethical will in the spirit of 1 Corinthians 15:3 ("I handed on to you as of first importance what I in turn had received") and pass it on to the people they love. Jesus actually does this for his disciples in the form of his final discourse in John 14–17.

Challenge your group members to take some time this week to write down the values, life lessons, and components of their faith that they would like to pass on to loved ones.

Thank everyone for having taken part in the study. Close the session by praying this prayer or one of your own:

Almighty God, we are grateful for the opportunity that we have had to study Paul's letter over the past six weeks and for the fellowship that we have enjoyed as we've grown in our faith together. May your Spirit continue to work in our hearts so that we might live, not by the wisdom of the world, but by the Logic of Love. Empower us to work through conflicts, treat each other with respect, lift up the gifts of our brothers and sisters, and let go of the nonessential things that distract us from your love. Amen.

CPSIA information can be obtained
at www.ICGtesting.com
Printed in the USA
LVHW041049290621
691388LV00004B/9